EARTH'S RESOURCES

GOLD
AND
SILVER

NEIL MORRIS

W
FRANKLIN WATTS
LONDON•SYDNEY

An Appleseed Editions book

First published in 2005 by Franklin Watts
96 Leonard Street, London, EC2A 4XD

Franklin Watts Australia
Level 17/207 Kent Street, Sydney, NSW 2000

© 2005 Appleseed Editions

Created by Appleseed Editions Ltd,
Well House, Friars Hill, Guestling, East Sussex,
TN35 4ET

Designed by Guy Callaby

ISBN 0 7496 5990 4

A CIP catalogue for this book is available from the
British Library.

Photographs by Corbis (AINACO, Paul Almasy,
Archivo Iconografico S.A., Asian Art & Archaeology,
Inc., Bettmann, José Manuel Sanchis Calvete,
Philippe Eranian, Peter M. Fisher, Michael Freeman,
Roger Garwood & Trish Ainslie, Paul Hardy, Peter
Harholdt, Dave G. Houser, YIORGOS KARAHALIS/
Reuters, Dan Lamont, Thom Lang, Michael S.
Lewis, Massimo Listri, Christophe Loviny, Maurice
Nimmo; Frank Lane Picture Agency, Greg Probst,
Charles O'Rear, Reuters, Royalty-Free, Anders
Ryman, Michael T. Sedam, Penny Tweedle, Roger
Wood, Adam Woolfitt), Getty Images (Stewart
Cohen, DIMITAR DILKOFF/AFP, Kevin Horan,
Michael Malyszko)

Printed in Thailand

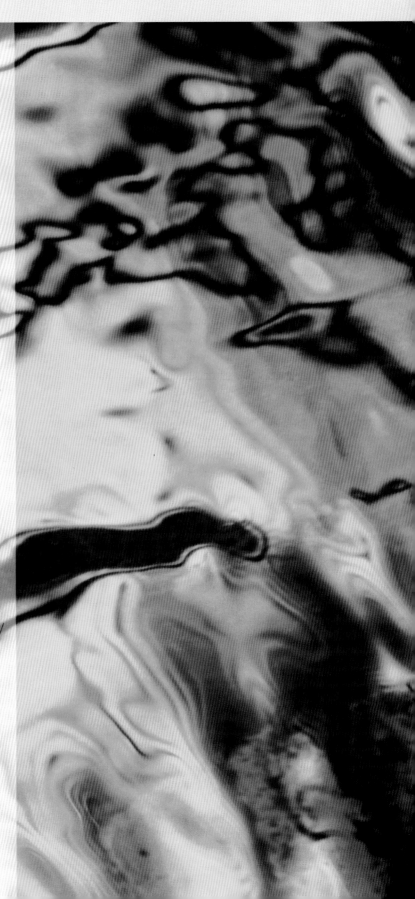

CONTENTS

INTRODUCTION

Gold and silver are the two metals that people have prized above all others since ancient times. Throughout history, people have found them both beautiful and useful, and they have been important trading items for thousands of years.

Gold has always been especially valued, perhaps because it is so scarce. Along with platinum, gold and silver have come to be known as precious metals. Scientists also call these three, together with mercury, noble metals. This is because they are the least reactive of all the world's metals: they do not react easily with the air or other substances and are not attacked by most acids. This means the noble metals do not corrode, keeping their beauty and usefulness. No wonder gold and silver are still the world's most popular metals for jewellery and fine ornaments. And they have many other uses too.

In sports, winners' medals are usually made of gold and runners-up are awarded silver. In the Olympic Games, both medals are actually made of silver, but the first-place medal is coated with pure gold. The bronze medal contains copper, zinc, tin, and a small amount of silver.

Au for gold

The chemical symbol for gold is Au, which comes from the Latin word for the metal *aurum*. Gold has a beautiful yellow colour, with a bright metallic glow. It is a very heavy metal – nearly 20 times as heavy as water – but it is also soft. This means that gold is easy to work and shape. It can be hammered into extremely thin sheets known as gold leaf. Gold can also be drawn into long, very thin wires without breaking. One troy ounce (31 grams) of gold can make a fine wire more than 100 kilometres long. These are very useful properties, and at the same time gold never goes dull, but keeps its bright, shiny colour.

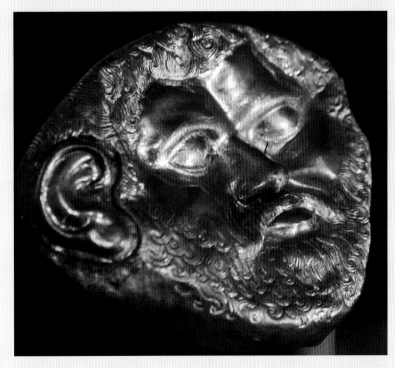

This mask of hammered gold was made by a craftsman of the ancient Thracian people, who lived in the region of present-day Bulgaria. The mask was made around 450 BC. and weighs 500 grams.

Ag for silver

Silver's chemical symbol is Ag, from the Latin word *argentum*. This metal has a white, shiny colour and is second only to gold in its ability to be hammered into shapes and drawn into fine wires. Silver is just over half as heavy as gold, and it is the best conductor of heat and electricity of all the metals. Unlike gold, however, it reacts with the sulphur compounds in polluted air and over time forms a black film of silver sulphide called tarnish.

This tarnished silver cutlery needs to be polished before being used. Despite its tarnish, the silver still reflects light well.

WHERE IN THE WORLD?

***G**old is found in very small quantities all over the world. It exists as tiny deposits in rocks that formed throughout Earth's history, from the earliest geological period. In most places there is too little of it to be worth recovering, but in a few locations it is found in concentrated amounts.*

The world's oceans also contain dissolved gold, but it is very difficult and extremely costly to extract reasonable quantities of the metal from seawater. On land, gold is often found combined with silver in an alloy called electrum, and both precious metals are also found as traces in rocks containing copper, lead or zinc. The world's leading producers of gold are South Africa, the United States and Australia. The largest producers of silver are Mexico, Peru and Australia. Altogether by weight, total world production of silver amounts to around seven times that of gold.

Gold bars and coins. The main international trading centre for precious metals is the London Bullion Market. Gold and silver are delivered there in bars and bought and sold in ounces.

Johannesburg

In 1886, an Australian farmer found a gold-bearing rock on his land in the Witwatersrand region of South Africa. Other finds followed, starting a gold rush to the area, with people coming from the US, Australia and Britain. The settlement near the goldfields was called Johannesburg, and in just 10 years, it grew into a city of 100,000 people. A British government official famously called it 'the richest place on Earth'. The area became the world's most important gold-producing region, and today the city has a population of nearly two million. It has two universities and in 1994 became the capital of the new South African province of Gauteng.

Johannesburg, known to mineworkers as eGoli – the City of Gold.

Some modern jewellers continue to work in a traditional way. This artist is making a silver pendant.

Pachuca

The city of Pachuca lies nearly 2,500 metres up in the Sierra Madre Oriental mountains, to the north of Mexico City. Spanish conquerors opened their first silver mine there in 1534. They realized that the region had been used as a source of the metal for many centuries before then, by the Aztecs and others. Today the hills around the city are riddled with old mines. The area still produces silver, and other metals are also mined, smelted and processed there.

SOURCES AND DEPOSITS

***B**oth gold and silver are sometimes found in deposits of so-called native metal. But finds of pure gold or silver are quite rare. It is much more common to discover deposits in rocks where precious metals are mixed with other minerals in ores or metal-bearing rocks.*

Both gold and silver often occur in ores containing sulphur compounds called sulphides. Scientists believe that all of these deposits were formed by hot liquid solutions being forced from deep underground into cracks in overlying cooler rocks. This movement is caused by the volcanic activity of molten rocks beneath Earth's crust or outer layer. As the liquid solutions cool, they form solid deposits in the cracks, leaving veins of precious metals.

Champagne Pool, in the Waiotapu thermal area of New Zealand, is a hot-water pool heated by underground volcanic activity. As water in the pool evaporates, it leaves behind traces of gold, silver and mercury.

Underground lodes

Lodes are the largest deposits of precious metals, where a number of veins of solid ore are found close together in what were once cracks in the rocks. Gold and silver lodes are most commonly found in ancient mountain ranges in various parts of the world. Geologists – scientists who study the structure of Earth – believe that some lodes were formed as long ago as 2.6 billion years. Throughout recent history, people have tried to make their fortune by looking for big lodes. Successful American examples are the mythical Mother Lode of gold, found in California in 1848, and the Comstock Lode of silver, discovered in Nevada in 1859.

You can see traces of gold in this quartz rock.

A handful of gold nuggets found in Australia.

Surface placers

Placer deposits of gold occur when a vein is exposed at the surface of the land. Over a period of time, the vein is worn away and small fragments are carried away by wind and water. Rain washes the loose gold, along with sand and gravel, into a stream which carries it downhill. But because gold is so heavy, it usually sinks to the bottom of the stream. Sometimes it builds up on sandbanks and islands in streams – forming a dream find for the gold prospector. But if it is left alone, over millions of years the gold may become buried again in newly formed rocks.

MINING

Precious metals and their ores are mined both underground and at the surface. Geologists and other scientists first survey a likely site, and experts make test drillings to check the quantity and quality of the ore and make sure that it is worth mining.

The tests also allow mining companies to decide which kind of mine is best and how deep they will need to dig. In underground mines, workers use drills to remove chunks of ore from the rock face. The ore is then taken away by electric railway cars and hoisted through shafts to the surface. Some mines have both underground and open-pit operations, and many companies mine for both gold and silver as well as other metals.

A worker drills for gold in South Africa, where a large mine can employ up to 16,000 workers. Gold makes up more than a third of the country's export earnings.

Open pits

Opencast or open-pit mining is used to recover precious metals from thick beds of ore that lie close to the surface. After test drilling, explosives are used to break up the surface rocks. Miners then operate mechanical shovels to dig the deposits in a series of horizontal layers called benches, which are usually about 10 metres thick. Roads connect the benches up the sides of the pit so that trucks can haul the ore to a processing plant. Open pits can become huge holes in the ground, but they do not last forever. For example, an opencast gold and silver mine was opened on the Pacific island of Misima in 1990. It closed in 2001 after producing 105 tonnes of gold and five times that amount of silver.

Panning and sluicing

Gold prospectors have traditionally searched for placer deposits by panning. They first look for a stream that might be carrying gold fragments away from a lode. Then they wash loose gravel and sand from the bottom of the stream in a shallow, round pan. Heavy gold particles are separated and stay in the middle of the pan. Some prospectors set up large sluice boxes, sending the material down a long chute so that gold settles in grooves at the bottom. This kind of mining is painstaking work, and commercial companies use large dredges instead to recover minerals from riverbeds.

 Trucks carry ore out of Goldstrike Mine, Nevada. Gold was first found in this region of the US in 1867.

These women are panning for gold in a river in Laos, in southeast Asia.

EXTRACTING AND REFINING

Underground and opencast mines often produce small quantities of native precious metals, but most gold and silver has to be extracted from ores.

These are first delivered to a treatment plant, where they are crushed and ground. The crushing machine contains a swinging weight, which smashes the rocks into smaller chunks. These travel along a conveyor belt to ball mills where steel balls move about inside a rotating drum and grind the small chunks into fine particles. In ancient times, gold-bearing ore was crushed by hand and then treated with mercury in a process called amalgamation. The mercury dissolved the gold, and the liquid amalgam was separated from the rock by squeezing it through leather bags. The amalgam was then heated so that the mercury boiled off and left the gold. Today, more complex chemical methods are used to recover the precious metal.

Powerful machines and mills reduce the ore to fine particles.

After many processing stages, the molten gold has been extracted from the ore.

Recovering gold

In many gold-processing plants, the crushed ore is treated with a solution of sodium cyanide. Grains of carbon are then added to this pulp, and the dissolved gold collects on the grains. Next, the carbon is treated with chemicals to release the gold solution, and the carbon grains are removed. The gold is then recovered from the solution by a process called electrowinning. An electric current is passed through the solution, and the gold is deposited on steel wool. Finally, the steel wool is smelted in a furnace, separating the molten gold, which is poured into moulds called ingots. Impurities are removed from the gold at a refinery.

Silver methods

Most silver is extracted from ores of copper and lead. After crushing and smelting, the ores release their combined metals. Silver is separated from copper by treating it with nitric acid and then recovering the precious metal by electrowinning. In the extraction process from lead ore, zinc is added to form an alloy with the silver, which is then removed from the zinc by heating. As with gold, the extracted silver is further purified and improved at a refinery.

The main silver-bearing ores of copper (chalcopyrite, left) and lead (galena).

IN ANCIENT TIMES

Historians believe that various ways of mining and using metals were discovered independently in different parts of the world. The first metals to be used were copper and gold, probably because they were found as nuggets and were soft enough to be hammered and shaped.

The world's oldest hoard of gold objects was found in an ancient burial ground at Varna, on the Black Sea in present-day Bulgaria. In 1972, archaeologists found hundreds of graves in which the bodies had been surrounded by items made of gold, copper, shell and stone. They were made more than 6,000 years ago. All of the ancient civilizations that emerged after this time – including those of the Egyptians, Minoans, Mycenaeans, Greeks, Romans and Celts – used gold and praised it as the most beautiful metal.

This gold cup comes from ancient Mesopotamia and was made in about the 12th century BC. It is decorated with winged bulls.

Symbol of eternity

The ancient Egyptians saw gold as a symbol of eternity, because it was the colour of the sun and was unaffected by time (since it did not tarnish). The Egyptians also revered silver, which was discovered later, and in rituals they came to regard gold as the flesh of the great sun-god Ra, covering the silver of his bones. Gold was used to make images of the god, and as gold leaf to cover other wooden statues. Masks and coffins were made of gold, such as those made famous by the discovery of the tomb of King Tutankhamen, who was mummified more than 3,000 years ago. Egyptian gold was mined in the Eastern Desert and in the southern region of Nubia. It helped make Egypt rich and was described around 1,359 BC as being 'as plentiful as dirt'!

 This golden mask was found covering the face of the mummy of Tutankhamen. It was made from two sheets of gold, which were hammered together, and the eyes are quartz and obsidian (volcanic glass). The mask weighs more than 10 kilograms.

Find at Mycenae

In 1876, famous German archaeologist Heinrich Schliemann discovered five royal graves in the ancient city of Mycenae, Greece. To his delight and amazement, the graves contained gold and silver objects as well as jewels and bronze weapons. Bronze daggers had golden handles, but the most remarkable finds were gold death masks. They had been made by beating sheets of gold over wooden moulds that had been carved to look like the king. The mask was then laid over the dead king's face before the grave was closed.

 This death mask from Mycenae is called the 'Mask of Agamemnon', but it was actually made for a different king, about 1,500 BC.

COINS AND CURRENCY

Gold and silver, along with copper, are often called the 'coinage metals'. Historians believe that the world's first coins were actually made of electrum, a natural mixture of gold and silver. They were made around 700 BC in ancient Lydia, part of present-day Turkey. Designs were stamped on them to show that the coins were all of the same value, saving traders the trouble of weighing each piece of precious metal.

The later Lydian king Croesus, who was famous for his great wealth, had separate gold and silver coins minted. The ancient Romans kept up this tradition, with gold coins weighing more and being more valuable than silver. This was the way most of the world's currencies worked for more than 2,000 years. During the 20th century, however, gold and silver were dropped in favour of less valuable metals. Today, most coins are made of copper, zinc, manganese and nickel, or alloys of these metals.

These electrum coins from ancient Lydia are called staters, meaning 'weights'. Their designs were stamped using a hammer and a die.

Imperial gold and silver

The ancient Romans used lumps of bronze as currency before they issued their first silver coins around 289 BC. Gold coins were introduced less than 100 years later. During imperial times, the minting of precious metals remained under the supervision of the emperor, while the Roman senate and individual cities were allowed to mint copper and bronze coins. Most emperors had their portrait and name stamped on the front of coins, with Roman symbols such as horses and chariots on the other side.

Front (left) and back (above) of Roman gold solidus coins, dating from AD 390-400.

The gold standard

During the 18th century, British bankers began defining the value of their currency – all metal coins and paper notes – in terms of gold. This meant that currency could always be exchanged for the precious metal, at least in theory. This system was known as the gold standard, and it was adopted by many countries in the following century. This set value in gold made international trade easier. Still, the gold standard was abandoned during the 20th century, and since the 1970s the price of gold has been allowed to float freely in an open market. This means that its value can go up and down.

Gold bars are stamped with their weight and a unique reference number.

SUN AND MOON

People have always been fascinated by the lasting quality of gold, the reflective quality of silver, and both metals' association with the universe and immortality. During the Middle Ages, alchemists believed that they could create precious metals, and in their attempts they made astrological links between the metals and the planets.

This golden teacup was made in China during the period of the Tang dynasty (A.D. 618-907).

Gold was associated with the sun, as it had been in ancient Egypt. Silver was seen as a representation of the moon, perhaps because they both reflect the sun's light so well. Since the heavenly bodies were thought to control the metals, alchemists believed that the position of the sun and moon could influence the success or failure of their work. In China, there was also a longheld belief that gold could cure illness. As a result, rich people preferred to eat from gold plates.

From base to precious metals

Medieval alchemists tried to change so-called base metals, such as lead or copper, into gold or silver. They considered gold to be the perfect metal and thought that if they could learn to make it, they could perfect many other things. These alchemists were scholars, philosophers and scientists, and they used laboratory apparatus and scientific experiments to try to discover the substance that could turn a base metal into a precious one. This mythical substance came to be known as the 'philosopher's stone'. They never did find it (modern scientists know that no such substance exists), but alchemists such as Paracelsus (1493-1541) gained a lot of chemical knowledge through their experiments. Their understanding of the way in which heat could be used to alter metals and other elements helped with the later science of chemistry.

The Alchemist's Laboratory *was painted in 1570.*

Would you be fooled by fool's gold? Most people are, but it's lighter and harder to shape than real gold. These pieces look like silver.

Fool's gold

Throughout history – and still today – people have found nuggets of a shiny yellow mineral in the ground and thought they had discovered gold. Unfortunately for them most had actually come across a similar mineral called pyrite, which is made up of iron and sulphur. It is quite common in rocks such as shale and limestone, and its deceptive appearance has given it the name 'fool's gold'. The name 'pyrite' comes from the Greek word for fire, because the mineral gives off sparks when it is struck and was therefore used for lighting fires. Today it is used commercially as a source of sulphur.

GOLD FEVER

There have been many instances in history when thousands of people have moved quickly to an area where gold has been found. The greatest gold rushes were in the US (the first in 1849), Australia (1851), New Zealand (1861), South Africa (1886), and Canada (1897).

During the Canadian gold rush, more than 30,000 people poured into the remote region of the Klondike River to dig for gold. The people of the modern-day town of Dawson celebrate Discovery Day every August 17th in memory of the first find on that day in 1896. History's biggest silver rush started in 1859, when the so-called Comstock Lode was discovered in Nevada. That year, the town of Virginia City was founded, and it soon had 30,000 inhabitants. Farther south, across Gold Hill, sprang up the community of Silver City.

Today the former silver bonanza town of Virginia City has few residents, but buildings have been preserved for tourists.

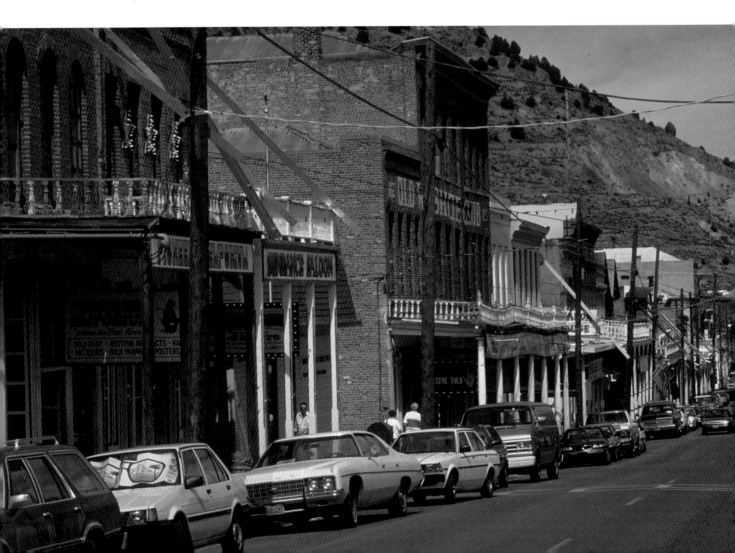

The Forty-Niners

One morning in 1848, James Marshall, who was building a sawmill beside the American River in California, saw a yellow nugget in a stream. It was gold and more finds soon spread the news far and wide. The following year, people poured in from across the continent in covered wagons and from around the world on steamships. These prospectors came to be known as the 'Forty-Niners' (from the year 1849), and California's population grew to nearly 100,000. The small port of San Francisco developed into a city, and by 1850 there were enough Californians for the region to be admitted to the Union as a state. California's nickname is the Golden State, and its official motto also celebrates the Forty-Niners: 'Eureka!' ('I have found it!').

Digging and panning for gold in California in 1871. Many prospectors who did not find gold stayed and became farmers.

On the golden trail

A travelling Englishman named Edward Hargraves left Australia in 1849 to join the California gold rush. Having failed to make his fortune, he returned to Australia and put his new-found prospecting knowledge to work. In 1851, he struck gold in a creek off the Macquarie River of New South Wales, starting the Australian gold rush. More finds were made in the colony of Victoria, and soon prospectors were flooding in from overseas to follow a 'golden trail' around the huge continent. During the 1850s, the Australian population more than doubled to well over a million people.

Prospectors pan for gold in New South Wales in 1852, just a year after the first discovery in Australia.

GOLDSMITHS AND SILVERSMITHS

During the Middle Ages, European craftsmen formed guilds, and goldsmiths made up one of the most respected of these associations. They worked in all precious metals, and in 1327 the Goldsmiths' Company received a royal charter, or written grant, from the King of England.

Every craftsman had to place a mark on his work and take it to Goldsmiths' Hall in London where the piece's purity was checked and stamped – this led to the stamps being called 'hallmarks'. Up to 1773, the penalty for counterfeiting a British hallmark was execution (today the crime carries 10 years' imprisonment). Hallmarks vary around the world, but most are symbols showing the maker, purity, assay (or approval) office and date of manufacture. Today, most goldsmiths are artists with their own studio workshops. Some also work as part-time industrial designers in factories that produce modern jewellery.

Stephen I was crowned King of Hungary on Christmas Day, 1000. It is said that this gold crown was sent by Pope Sylvester II, and it later became a Hungarian national treasure. The crown was taken to the US during World War II but returned in 1978.

24-carat jewellery

Since ancient times, gold has been the most prized metal for making jewellery. In recent centuries, the purer the gold, the more valuable the jewellery. Gold purity is measured in carats. Pure gold has 24 carats, so 18-carat gold is three-quarters pure (with the other quarter being a different metal), and 12-carat is half pure. So-called 'white gold' contains nickel, and 'red gold' is an alloy with copper. The fineness of gold is also expressed in parts of a thousand, so '750 fine' is the same as 18-carat gold. Jewellery made of '990 gold' is mixed with 1 per cent titanium.

This Kuna woman from Panama wears handmade gold rings.

Sterling silver

Most high-quality silver jewellery and cutlery is made of sterling silver, which is made up of 92.5 per cent silver and 7.5 per cent copper. The copper increases the silver's hardness and strength. The name 'sterling' has been used since the 13th century, when the English imported silver coins from eastern Europe, calling them 'easterlings' and marking them with a little star (or 'sterling'). Like gold, the fineness of silver is also given in parts of a thousand, so sterling is '925 fine'. Less expensive silver plate has been made since the 18th century by coating copper, and later steel, with a thin layer of silver. Since 1840, this coating has also been applied by electroplating, and silverware marked 'EPNS' is electroplated nickel silver.

Sterling silver is popular for high-quality tea and coffee sets. Unfortunately, silver tarnishes so the pieces have to be polished regularly.

USEFUL RESOURCE

Precious metals have many uses in addition to currency and jewellery. Both gold and silver are used by dentists for fillings as amalgams with other metals such as mercury, tin and copper. Gold also has many high-tech applications, because it reflects heat, light and radiation so well.

Gold-coated plastic film is useful for protecting spacecraft from the sun's rays; for the same reason, it is applied as a wafer-thin film to the windows of jet aircraft. In buildings, the use of a transparent gold film in glass means that windows can reflect heat without reducing light, keeping office workers cool in the summer. Silver has a special use in photographic film, and silver oxide is used to make small, powerful batteries for calculators and watches.

Gold film was used on the lunar module, and its use on astronauts' visors protects them from solar radiation.

Gold-plated contacts

Gold is the best metal to use for small electronic contacts, switches and other components. This is because it conducts electricity very well but does not corrode or tarnish, even at very high temperatures. Such electronic parts are used in computers, televisions, and telephones. Because gold is costly, it is normally applied as a very thin film over other metals to make gold-plated contacts. Thin gold wire is also widely used in the electronics industry to connect different parts. A solid-gold wire (up to 999.9 fine) may be as thin as 1/100th of a millimetre.

Gold-plated contacts are an essential part of many kinds of modern electronic equipment.

This is what photographic film looks like after it has received an image inside a camera and been developed with special chemicals.

Photographic film

Some silver compounds are light-sensitive, which means they change to metallic silver when exposed to light. Most photographic film is made of a layer of emulsion spread on a plastic base. The emulsion contains grains of silver bromide, and different parts of each exposure change according to the amount of light thrown on to them. The areas that are exposed to light get darker, making a negative image (with light areas dark). This is then turned back to positive, with the light areas light-coloured, as a print is made of the picture on photographic paper that is also coated with a silver-based, light-sensitive emulsion.

MYTHS AND LEGENDS

Precious metals, and especially gold, have played a major role in countless legendary tales. Many are based on metals or other objects turning to gold, or on daring adventures undertaken to find hidden treasure.

One such tale was part of German and Scandinavian folklore that inspired a 13th-century epic poem and a 19th-century opera by Richard Wagner. The tale concerns the Nibelungs, a race of dwarfs who steal a hoard of gold from the Rhine maidens. One of the dwarfs makes a gold ring that gives magical powers to whoever wears it but also causes chaos. In other legends, silver often appears as a happy omen, and to this day silver coins are thought of as lucky (even if they are not really made of silver!)

The Rhine maidens guard their golden treasure in the ancient German tale of the Nibelungs.

The Midas touch

According to an ancient Greek myth, Midas was king of Phrygia, a country in Asia Minor (modern Turkey). Granted a single wish by the god Dionysus, Midas asked that all he touched should turn to gold. The wish was granted, and at first Midas was delighted when he touched his chair and table and their wood instantly turned into solid gold. But when he was hungry, the king found that all the food he touched also turned to gold. When he asked to undo the wish, he was told to wash in the Pactolus (modern Gediz) River. In ancient times, people found grains of gold in the river, and the Midas legend was given as an explanation. Today, people are said to have the 'Midas touch' when they make money in everything they do.

When King Midas touched his daughter, he was horrified to see that she also turned to gold.

El Dorado

In the 16th century, Spanish adventurers heard tales of a Native American king who was fabulously wealthy. According to the tales, the king had gold dust sprinkled on his skin every day. He would then sail out on to a lake on a raft and throw gold into the depths to please his sun god. The Spaniards called him El Dorado (the 'golden man') and went in search of him. Some heard rumours that the legendary kingdom was beside Lake Guatavita, in present-day Colombia. But the kingdom was never found.

Lake Guatavita was partially drained in the 16th century and completely emptied three centuries later. Tiny amounts of gold were found, but not enough to solve the mystery of El Dorado.

TODAY AND TOMORROW

*T*he volume of the world's underground reserves of precious metals is unknown, and experts are constantly looking for new sources all over the world. At the same time, the demand for gold and silver remains high. The two metals will surely always be popular for jewellery, and they are finding new industrial uses all the time, especially in the field of electronics.

But we are becoming more and more aware that mining and industrial processes have a vast impact on the environment, and many governments are trying to make the extraction of precious metals much less damaging to wild habitats and local communities. Some environmentalists say this is particularly important because jewellery is a non-essential product. But as we have seen, precious metals have many other uses besides jewellery, and more may be found in the future in fields such as electronics and space travel.

Precious metals are traditionally used in beautiful ways. This bride in Thailand wears a necklace of silver.

Searching for gold, prospectors found silver-bearing ore in the Bunker Hill region in 1885. More than 100 years later, work was underway to clean up the surrounding region.

The number of recycling centres is growing as people come to realize the cumulative value of tiny amounts of precious metals.

Clean-up sites

Until the late 20th century, mining and processing companies were much less aware than they are today that their activities were threatening the environment. At the Bunker Hill mine in Idaho, for example, ore waste was dumped straight into a nearby river until 1968. The polluted river became dangerous for humans and wildlife, and since then the US Environmental Protection Agency has been working to clean up the area around the mine, known as Silver Valley. In many parts of the world, attempts are being made to better protect the environment from the effects of mining.

Recycling gold

Because of its great value, gold is one of few metals to have been recycled throughout history. Much modern jewellery contains gold that was first mined many centuries ago and has been smelted and re-cast. Some people sell old jewellery that they inherit, and this can be made into more modern items that people want to buy. In recent years, recycling plants have recovered more and more scrap-metal gold from electronic devices such as computers.

GLOSSARY

alchemy An early form of chemistry, which included attempts to change base metals into gold.

alloy A mixture of two or more metals.

amalgam A mixed paste of different metals that quickly hardens.

amalgamation A method of extracting gold from ore by using mercury to form an amalgam with the metal.

archaeologist A person who studies the ancient past by digging up and looking at remains.

assay office The place where precious metals are tested and approved.

base metal A common, non-precious metal.

bullion Gold or silver in bulk (usually bars or ingots).

carat A unit of measurement of the purity of gold.

conductor A substance that allows electricity or heat to pass through it.

corrode To be slowly destroyed by chemical action.

crust Earth's outer layer.

currency A system of money.

die A metal tool on a stamping machine.

dredge A machine with a revolving chain of buckets that digs material from riverbeds.

electrowinning The process of extracting metal from a solution by passing an electric current through it.

electrum A natural alloy of gold and silver.

emulsion A thin coating of silver bromide on photographic film or paper.

environmentalist A person who is concerned about and acts to protect the natural environment.

extract To take out or obtain something from a source.

geological period A long period of time in the history of Earth.

geologist A scientist who studies the structure of the Earth.

gold leaf A very thin sheet of gold.

gold rush A wave of migration to a region because gold has been found there.

gold standard The system by which the value of a currency was defined in terms of gold.

goldfield An area where gold is found and mined.

gold-plated Having a thin coating of gold.

goldsmith A person who makes gold articles.

guild An association of merchants or craftsmen.

hallmark A mark stamped on gold and silver articles to show their standard of purity.

ingot A rectangular mould used for casting metals.

lode A large deposit of a precious metal or ore.

native metal A metal found in a pure state.

noble metal One of the least reactive metals – gold, silver, platinum or mercury.

nugget A small lump of gold or silver.

opencast or **open-pit mine** A mine in which ore is extracted at or near the surface of the earth.

ore Rock or mineral containing a useful metal.

placer A deposit of sand and gravel (for example, on the bed of a river) that contains particles of precious metals.

pollute To damage with harmful substances.

precious metal One of the valuable metals – gold, silver or platinum.

prospector Someone who explores an area in search of precious metals.

reactive Describing a metal that reacts easily with the air or another substance (and corrodes).

recycle To process used material so that it can be used again.

silver plate Articles made of a base metal coated with a thin layer of silver.

silversmith A person who makes silver articles.

sluice box A box connected to a water chute; it is used to collect fragments of gold.

smelt To heat and melt ore to get metal from it.

solar radiation Rays of energy from the sun.

sterling silver High-quality silver that is 92.5 per cent pure.

tarnish A discolouring, black film that forms on silver.

trace A very small quantity.

troy ounce A unit of weight used for precious metals and gems.

vein A layer (of metal or ore) formed in a crack between rocks.

INDEX